MY VEGGETTI SPIRAL VEGETABLE CUTTER RECIPE BOOK

FOR EASY PALEO, GLUTEN-FREE AND WEIGHT LOSS DIETS!

Written by
J.S. Amie

www.HealthyHappyFoodie.org

Copyright © 2014 Healthy Happy Foodie Press

ISBN-13: 978-1500626051
ISBN-10: 1500626058

This book is for entertainment purposes. The publisher and author of this book are not reponsible in any manner whatsoever for any adverse effects arising directly or indirectly as a result of the information provided in this book.

INTRODUCTION

I wrote this book because I found very little in the way of recipes and basic "how to" instructions when I bought my first Veggetti Spiral Vegetable Cutter. I also noticed that a lot of people were having difficulties choosing the right vegetables, or handling the cutter correctly (if you use it correctly, you won't get cut!). And, I noticed there weren't enough recipes to keep my family craving more!

So, after using the Veggetti cutter myself, getting familiar with the proper way to use it, and testing all sorts of recipes to find the best ones, I put together this handy manual / recipe book to help people like you get the most they can out of their new Veggetti cutter.

The Veggetti cutter is an extremely useful tool to have in your kitchen. Now that you have one, read this book, go forth, and multiply your deliciousness!

WHO THIS BOOK IS FOR

The Veggetti Spiral Vegetable Cutter was made to help people live healthier lives by decreasing wheat in their diets and by increasing the amount of vegetables they eat Anyone who is trying to cut wheat out of his or her diet will immediately see the possibilities that open up when you have the ability to make your own delicious pasta substitute.

The Veggetti cutter is perfect for food lovers on any kind of regimen, including gluten-free, Paleo or a weight loss diets. This book will not only give you great recipes to utilize your Veggetti cutter, but it will show you how to use this utensil safely and efficiently.

Besides the flattering compliments you'll receive for the new flavors and textures you serve, you'll also be cooking much healthier meals. Instead of pasta and other wheat-based dishes, you'll be serving hearty vegetables that have the same look and texture of those ingredients that you're cutting out of your diet.

***

TABLE OF CONTENTS

HOW TO SAFELY USE
YOUR VEGGETTI CUTTER

This inventive kitchen utensil is a no brainer. It's easy to use, but it can bite if you're not careful.

The blades are super sharp, so you do need to be alert while you're turning your vegetables into delicious, low calorie spaghetti strands. *Since the blades are so incredibly sharp, that means you don't need to force the zucchini or carrot through the cutter.* All you do is gently guide them through.

Here's how to use it safely:

STEP 1: Peel 2/3 of the skin off the carrot or zucchini. Always leave the skin on where your hand will be holding the vegetable. The skin reduces the risk of your hand slipping and getting cut on the Veggetti cutter blades. Most people get cut because they don't pay attention to what they're doing and because their fingers slide down the damp vegetable toward the blades. Make sure to pay attention, and use the Veggetti cutter cap that fits on the end of the vegetable where your hand guides the zucchini into the cutter.

NOTE: The cap comes with the Veggetti cutter for a purpose. It gives you extra leverage to guide the vegetable and it protects your fingers from being cut by the blades inside the cutter. Using the cap is part of the process. You can also use a straight fork stuck into the end where your hand guides the vegetable. This serves the same purpose as the cap and may allow for even more of the vegetable to be pasta-ized.

STEP 2: Once you peel part of your zucchini and put the Veggetti cutter cap on the pushing end, you are ready to go. Gently slide the zucchini into the tunnel of the cutter and begin turning the vegetable, just like a pencil sharpener. As soon as the turning starts you'll see the strands of vegetable "pasta" coming out of the Veggetti. Most people just spiral cut the peeled part of the zucchini or carrot or whatever, and discard or slice up the unpeeled piece. You would only be endangering your fingers if you attempt to push the unpeeled or short left over part of the zucchini or carrot into the Veggetti.

NOTE: *There are two different sized blades at either end of the cutter. One side will give you thicker "pasta" and the other will give you thinner "pasta".*

***

HOW TO CLEAN
YOUR VEGGETTI CUTTER

Cleaning is a snap, although you do have to be extra careful of the sharp blades and the miniscule pieces of vegetable residue stuck between the blades. Many people recommend the sink power sprayer to force these particles out, and some Veggetti cutter users overwhelmingly suggest just tossing the Veggetti cutter into the dishwasher where it belongs. Both methods are sound and both methods work.

However, some very astute Veggetti cutter lovers came up with a most inventive idea that seems to be catching on quickly. A toothbrush. A BRAND NEW, CLEAN TOOTHBRUSH. New toothbrushes are cheap and available for a dollar or less in many places. Use a medium hardness brush and you'll be able to brush any particles out of the cutter blades in seconds. The toothbrush will save your fingers and keep you assured of a constantly clean Veggetti cutter machine.

***

WHAT ARE THE BEST VEGETABLES TO USE?

Zucchini

A medium sized zucchini is abundant in Vitamin A and C, has over 2 grams of protein, 2 grams of fiber and 6 grams of carbohydrates. It's an antioxidant and among other things, can help lower your cholesterol levels and has only 33 calories.

Carrots

A medium sized carrot has only 52 calories, 12 grams of carbohydrates, 4 grams of fiber and is one of the best natural sources of vitamin A. Carrots also contain iron, B6 and other B vitamins, manganese, vitamin E, K and C, along with phosphorus, choline, potassium and calcium.

Radishes

Radishes are great little antioxidant treats. They're full of vitamin C, which can help the immune system, along with building and maintaining bones, teeth, blood vessels and tissues. They also contain B and K vitamins, potassium, calcium, manganese, iron, phosphorus, zinc and copper. Radishes are also cancer fighters because of their isothiocyanate compounds, and they are an extremely low calorie and low carb gem of a snack.

Potatoes

Potatoes are low in calories, only about a hundred for a medium sized one. They are also full of fiber, vitamin C, B6 and other B vitamins, and a great deal of vitamin A. The minerals in a potato are potassium, phosphorus, calcium and magnesium, which aid the body in bone building. Potatoes are great as immune system boosters, vision improvers and bone builders.

Beets

Beets, (both the roots and the greens are edible), are vitamin rich, especially in the B complex vitamins, along with A and C. These low calorie, high fiber and zero cholesterol roots are also highly potent in minerals, such as, iron, potassium, magnesium, copper and manganese. The beet is also known as a great antioxidant and coronary artery protectorant, which can lower the rick of stroke and heart disease.

NOTE: Don't' forget…beautiful and edible garnishes can also be made from each of these vegetables.

***

HOW TO PREPARE
YOUR "VEGETABLE PASTA"

Cooking or preparing your vegetable pasta is even easier than real pasta. Here's how:

RAW

The "pasta" you make from cutting Zucchini, carrots and radishes can be eaten raw. Simply put the vegetable "pasta" in your plate and serve with the accompanying sauce or other ingredients shown in the following recipes.

WARMED

You can also warm up the vegetable "pasta" by placing in hot water for a few seconds, or simply microwave it for a few seconds.

BOILED

My favorite way to cook vegetable pasta is to boil it with just a little water. Just throw it in a pan with a about 1" of water (so it doesn't drown the veggies), and boil for a few minutes until the texture and firmness is to your taste.

TIP: if you undercook it just a little, then drizzle with virgin olive oil, you'll never want to cook it any other way.

SAUTEED

Another great way to prepare your vegetable "pasta" is to Sautee it in butter or olive oil. Be sure not to overcook it! Usually a few short minutes is all it takes.

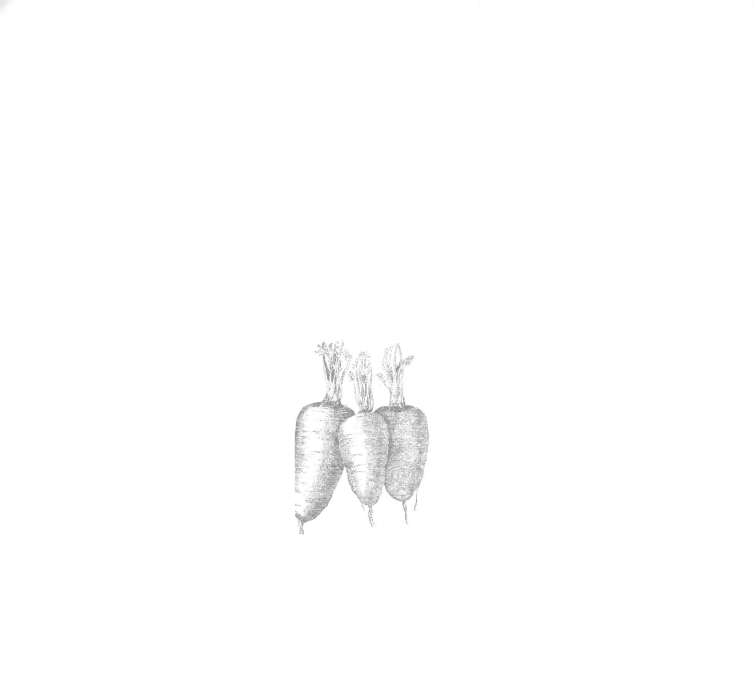

RECIPES TO MAKE
YOUR MOUTH WATER!

GENERAL RECIPES
(WITH NO DIET RESTRICTIONS)

Creamy Zucchini Pasta with Chicken

Ingredients:

- "PASTA"
  - 2 zucchinis (large)
- CHICKEN & SAUCE
  - 2 cloves garlic (minced)
  - ½ small onion (chopped)
  - 1 large head (600g) cauliflower, roughly chopped
  - ½ tsp sea salt
  - 1½ cups chicken stock
  - ½ tsp freshly cracked black pepper
  - ¾ cup mushrooms (sliced)
  - 1½ tbsp white balsamic vinegar

- ½ tbsp Dijon mustard
- 1 tbsp nutritional yeast
- juice of 1/2 lime
- 1 tsp capers
- ½ lb. cooked chicken, chopped

. . . .

Instructions:

- Make "pasta" strands out of the zucchini with your Veggetti. This recipe works with raw, warmed, blanched or sauteed vegetable pasta. Try them all!

- Add salt and pepper, garlic and onion to a saucepan and cook over medium heat for four to six minutes, until the fragrance becomes abundant and the mixture is soft when stirred.

- Toss the cauliflower in and cook for another two to 4 minutes.

- Pour in the chicken stock, and bring to a boil. Cover and reduce heat and let simmer until cauliflower is tender, about 5-7 minutes.

- Sauté the mushrooms in a large pan until golden brown. Then add the chicken and cook until heated thoroughly.

- Put the cauliflower mixture into the blender, then add the mustard, nutritional yeast, balsamic vinegar and lime juice and blend until smooth. Toss in capers and blend just a bit more to break them down. Pour cauliflower mixture over the chicken and mushrooms and simmer over low-medium heat.

- Put the zucchini pasta on a plate and drizzle the chicken sauce on top.

Pasta-Pizza

Ingredients:

- "PASTA"
  - 2 zucchinis (large)
  - 2 large carrots
- PIZZA SAUCE
  - 2 Italian chicken sausages (precooked and cut into small pieces)
  - 14 oz. of pizza sauce
  - 1 cup yellow onion (diced)
  - 1 cup mushrooms (diced)
  - 1 bell pepper (diced)
  - 1/4 cup black olives (sliced)
  - 4 garlic cloves (minced)
  - 1 tsp olive oil

Instructions:

- Make "pasta" strands out of the zucchini with your Veggetti. Heat or cook as you prefer.
- Heat olive oil, garlic and onions in a pan on medium heat until the onions are translucent. Then toss in the onions, pepper and mushrooms and cook for 4 – 6 minutes while mixing thoroughly.
- Add the precooked sausage pieces and stir for 3 -4 four minutes, enough to heat the sausage and blend the flavors.
- The pizza sauce is next. Add that to the mix and stir as everything heats up for another 2 to 4 minutes.
- You're done and now you can enjoy the taste and texture of pizza without the weight gain and discomfort that wheat crusts provide.

Pasta — Cajun Style

Ingredients:

- "PASTA"
  - 4 large zucchinis
- CAJUN SAUCE
  - ½ red bell pepper (chopped)
  - ½ green bell pepper (chopped)
  - 3 tbsp extra virgin olive oil
  - 2 garlic cloves (crushed)
  - ¼ yellow onion (chopped)
  - 8 oz. raw shrimp (cleaned)
  - 2 hot Italian sausages (or your choice of flavor and type, ½ inch cuts)
  - ½ cup coconut milk (canned is ok)
  - 4 tsp Cajun Spice Mix

Instructions:

- Make "pasta" strands out of the zucchini with your Veggetti. Heat or cook as you prefer.
- In a large pan, heat the olive oil over a medium heat. Then throw in the garlic, onion pieces and peppers, along with a tsp of Cajun Spice Mix. Cook these until they are tender, then transfer them to a bowl.
- Place the shrimp in the pan (add more olive oil if needed), and cook with another tsp of Cajun Spice Mix until they are pink, then remove from pan and put in bowl.
- Add sausage pieces, along with a tsp of Cajun Spice Mix to pan and sauté until thoroughly cooked, then put in bowl.
- Place "pasta" in pan, with the coconut milk and another tsp of Cajun Spice Mix and add more salt, pepper or cayenne if necessary. Mix together as it heats up.
- When thoroughly blended, pour this great tasting New Orleans sauce over the ingredients in the side bowl and mix well. Then…serve and enjoy.

Chicken Parmesan with Noodles

Ingredients:

....

- "PASTA"
  - 3 large zucchinis
- CHICKEN PARMESAN
  - 2 eggs
  - 1 cup walnuts
  - ½ cup ground Parmesan cheese
  - Italian seasoning
  - 3 boneless chicken breasts
  - 4-6 oz. tomato paste
  - 2 tbsp olive oil
  - 8 oz. pizza sauce
  - ½ cup mozzarella cheese (grated)
  - Italian seasoning (to taste)

....

Instructions:

- Make "pasta" strands out of the zucchini with your Veggetti. Heat or cook as you prefer.
- Preheat oven to 350° F.
- Chop 1 cup of walnuts in a food processor until pieces are small, then pour into a large bowl. Add Parmesan cheese to walnuts, then add pepper, salt and Italian seasoning.
- Cut Chicken breasts in thirds and dip them in whipped eggs, then into the walnut mix for a coating.
- In a non-stick pan, with olive oil, heat the chicken over medium heat and brown on both sides.
- Mix pizza sauce with the tomato paste. Place the chicken pieces on a cookie sheet and top with the mixed sauce and Mozzarella cheese for 25 to 30 minutes. Make sure the interior of the chicken is at least 165° F before

eating.

- When done, serve the chicken pieces on top of the warm "pasta" and you will be dining in heaven for a change. This meal will melt in your mouth and it will be one that's hard to forget.

Shrimp, Feta, Olives & Zucchini Pasta

Ingredients:

- "PASTA"
  - 3 large zucchinis
- SAUCE
  - ½ lb. medium shrimp (peeled and deveined)
  - 1 garlic clove (minced)
  - 2 tbsp olive oil
  - 12 oz. ounce crushed tomatoes (canned is okay)
  - ½ onion (chopped)
  - ½ head fennel (cored and thinly sliced)
  - ¼ cup green olives (pitted and chopped)
  - ¼ cup white wine
  - 1 tbsp oregano
  - ¼ cup feta (crumbled)

Instructions:

- Make "pasta" strands out of the zucchini with your Veggetti. Blanche or boil to taste. Drain and save 1 cup of the water for later.
- Heat 1 tbsp olive oil in large pan over medium heat and add shrimp. Cook for 3 to 5 minutes, or until they are pink in the middle. Put shrimp on plate and set aside.
- Put the remaining oil in the pan and add onion, garlic and fennel, salting and peppering to taste. Cook for 5 minutes or until brown.
- Stir in the tomatoes and wine and simmer for 5 to 7 minutes.
- Next, add the olives, pasta and shrimp, along with the extra cup of water that you saved earlier. Heat and stir for 3 to 5 minutes, then serve with oregano and feta as toppings.

Chicken, Veggies & Pesto Pasta

Ingredients:

- "PASTA"
  - 2 large zucchinis
- SAUCE
  - ½ lb. chicken breast (boneless skinless, cut into 1-inch pieces)
  - ½ cup Parmesan (shredded)
  - ½ cup artichoke hearts (quartered)
  - 6 oz. asparagus (trimmed & cut into 1/2-inch pieces)
  - ½ cup parsley (chopped)
  - 2 tbsp pine nuts
  - 2 tbsp olive oil
  - 1/3 cup white wine
  - 1 garlic clove (chopped)
  - 1/8 tsp salt
  - ½ tsp lemon juice
  - ½ tsp lemon zest
  - 2 tbsp water
  - 2/3 cup peas
  - 1/8 tsp black pepper (to taste)
  - ¼ onion (chopped)

Instructions:

- Boil the "pasta" made with your Veggetti cutter, for 4 to 6 minutes or until soft. Drain and set aside 1½ cups of the pasta water for later.
- In the blender, thoroughly liquefy the pine nuts, garlic, and a pinch of salt and 1 tbsp of oil.
- Then add parsley, water and Parmesan and pulse the blender about five times to combine the ingredients. Add the lemon zest to this mixture and

stir it in.

- Heat 1 tbsp of oil in a large pan and after seasoning the chicken with salt and pepper, put it into the pan and cook for 5 minutes over medium heat until brown all over. Put chicken on a plate and set aside.

- Now, add onion to the pan on medium heat and cook for 3 minutes, until it is limp. Then stir in the artichoke pieces and cook another 3 minutes. Add the wine and cook for 2 minutes more.

- The asparagus goes in to the pan next and that will be cooked for approximately 2 minutes, until tender/crisp.

- Now you can add the "pasta" plus the water that you saved and then add in the chicken, peas and pesto. Cook this mixture until the peas are done, about 1 to 2 minutes, and then drizzle the lemon juice in and stir. You are ready to serve.

Pasta with Roasted Red Peppers, Walnuts & Goat Cheese

Ingredients:

- "PASTA"
  - 2 large zucchinis
  - 1 large carrot
- SAUCE
  - 3 oz. goat cheese (crumbled)
  - 2 roasted red peppers (chopped)
  - 2 garlic cloves (sliced thinly)
  - 2 tbsp olive oil
  - 2 tbsp tomato paste
  - ¼ onion (chopped)
  - ½ tsp red pepper flakes
  - 1/3 cup walnuts (toasted & chopped)
  - 1 tsp sugar (or alternative sweetener)
  - ½ tsp salt
  - 1 tbsp thyme (fresh)

Instructions:

- Make "pasta" strands out of the zucchini with your Veggetti. Heat or cook as you prefer.
- Heat olive oil in a pan over medium heat and add onion and garlic and cook for about 5 minutes, or until they are soft.
- Stir in the roasted red peppers, and sweetener, along with the tomato paste and cook for 2 to 4 minutes, until the sauce thickens.
- Pour these pan ingredients into a blender and liquefy until texture is smooth.
- Reheat pan over medium flame and cook the pepper flakes and thyme for

about 1 minute.

- Throw in your "pasta" and add the red pepper liquid and a little salt to the pan. Combine by stirring.
- Add the water you saved from earlier and cook ingredients for about 2 minutes, until the sauce coats the "pasta."
- After topping this luscious treat of a meal with goat cheese and walnuts, it will be ready to serve.

Pasta with Clams

Ingredients:

- "PASTA"
  - 2 large zucchinis
  - 1 large carrot
- SAUCE
  - ½ lb. littleneck clams (these are the smallest clams)
  - 1 garlic clove (chopped)
  - 12 oz. spicy tomato sauce
  - 2 tbsp olive oil
  - 1 tbsp basil (chopped)
  - ¼ cup white wine

Instructions:

- Clean clams with a sanitized scrub brush to get rid of any sand or dirt. Dry with paper towels and store in refrigerator.
- Make "pasta" strands out of the zucchini with your Veggetti. Heat or cook as you prefer.
- Over medium heat, add garlic and olive oil to a large pan and cook until fragrant, but not yet brown, about 1 minute.
- Next, add the white wine, and bring it to a boil.
- Add the clams, cover, and cook for 5 to 7 minutes until they open. When they do open up, remove pan from heat and take out the shellfish, throwing away any unopened clams.
- Save the liquid and strain it.
- Heat the strained liquid and tomato sauce in a different pan, over medium heat. Combine the clams and basil with the tomato sauce mixture and pour over your vegetable "pasta" and serve.

Pasta with Charred Tomato Sauce

Ingredients:

- "PASTA"
  - 1 large zucchini
- SAUCE
  - 2 tomatoes (diced)
  - 7 garlic cloves (minced)
  - 1 ½ tbsp olive oil
  - ¼ onion (chopped
  - 5 basil leaves (chopped)
  - 3 tbsp ricotta cheese (part-skim)
  -)¼ eggplant (diced)

Instructions:

- Make "pasta" strands out of the zucchini with your Veggetti.
- Preheat oven to 325° and wrap 5 garlic cloves in aluminum foil, along with a pinch of salt and a ½ tsp of olive oil. Bake these for 40 to 50 minutes, or until nice and brown and the texture is soft.
- Use the other 1 tbsp of oil in a pan and sautee the diced eggplant for 10 to 12 minutes or until soft, then set eggplant aside on a dish.
- In the same pan, cook 2 garlic cloves, the diced tomatoes and onion, in a little olive oil for 2 to 4 minutes, turning once or twice.
- Liquefy these ingredients in a blender until they become paste-like in consistency, then set aside in a separate bowl.
- Mix the crushed pepper and salt along with the ricotta cheese, in another separate bowl.
- Cook the tomatoes over medium heat in a pan for 4 to 6 minutes, then add the eggplant, "pasta" and the garlic and the juices and stir to combine.
- Sprinkle basil over the mixture just before serving, along with dollops of the ricotta.

Lemon Chard Pasta

Ingredients:

- "PASTA"
  - 1 large zucchini
- SAUCE
  - 1 bunch Swiss chard (cut into 1/2-inch pieces)
  - 1 carrot (large)
  - 1/2 cup olives (pitted and chopped)
  - 1/8 cup cilantro (fresh, chopped)
  - 1 tbsp olive oil
  - 1 tsp apple cider vinegar
  - 1 scallions (sliced thinly)
  - 1/4 tsp paprika
  - 1 tsp lemon zest
  - 1 tbsp lemon juice
  - 1/4 tsp black pepper
  - 1/4 tsp salt

Instructions:

- Make "pasta" strands out of the zucchini with your Veggetti. Heat or cook as you prefer.
- In a pan, over medium heat, cook the chard in olive oil until limp, 4 to 6 minutes. Take out of pan and put in a good size serving bowl.
- Add the olives, cilantro, vinegar, and scallions, lemon zest, salt and pepper and the pasta, and toss to coat every ingredient.
- Add cooked pasta, olives, cilantro, scallions, vinegar, lemon juice, lemon zest, paprika, salt, and pepper, and gently toss to combine.

Pasta & Chia Meatballs

Ingredients:

- "PASTA"
  - 1 large zucchini
- MEATBALLS
  - 1 lb. ground beef (or turkey)
  - 4 tbsp tomato paste
  - 2 tbsp chia seeds
  - 3 cloves garlic (minced)
  - 2 tsp oregano
  - 2 tsp basil
  - 2 tsp avocado oil (for sautéing)
  - 1 tsp black pepper
  - 1 tsp salt
- MARINARA
  - 1 medium onion (diced)
  - 1 clove garlic (crushed)
  - 1 sprig of fresh rosemary (chopped)
  - ¼ cup lemon juice
  - ½ cup chicken stock
  - 1 can diced tomatoes (12 oz)
  - 1 can tomato sauce (12 oz.)
  - ½ tsp salt
  - ½ tsp. black pepper

Instructions:

- "PASTA"
  - Make "pasta" strands out of the zucchini. This recipe works with raw,

warmed, blanched or sauteed vegetable pasta. Try them all!

- CHIA MEATBALLS
  - Except the avocado oil, mix all ingredients in a bowl thoroughly. Let sit for 10 minutes.
  - Over medium heat, heat a good size pan and add the avocado oil.
  - Shape 8 meatballs and cook in pan until brown, turning at least 3 times.
  - When meatballs are almost fully cooked, place meatballs on a plate. You'll finish cooking meatballs shortly in the sauce. Empty all but 2 tbsp of oil from pan.
- MARINARA:
  - Add onion pieces to the pan and sauté about 3-5 minutes, until translucent.
  - Add rosemary and garlic and cook 2 to 4 minutes.
  - Add lemon juice and chicken stock, then the diced tomatoes, tomato sauce, salt, pepper, and mix well. Simmer over medium heat until sauce begins to thicken, about 20 minutes.
  - Reduce heat to low and gingerly add meatballs to the pan. Cook 10 minutes, or until meatballs are cooked thoroughly. That means no pink inside the meatballs.

When all is ready, you can lay down a foundation of "pasta" on a plate and top it with the fabulous chia meatballs that you just made and then cover all that with your homemade marinara sauce. Enjoy!

***

RECIPES FOR A WEIGHT LOSS DIET

Quick Spaghetti with Meat Sauce

Ingredients:

- "PASTA"
  - 2 large zucchinis
  - 1 large carrots
- SAUCE
  - ½ yellow onion (chopped)
  - ½ celery stalk (chopped)
  - 2 garlic cloves (crushed)
  - ½ lb. lean turkey or beef
  - 1 tbsp Italian seasoning
  - 12 oz. crushed tomatoes (canned is ok)
  - ½ tsp salt
  - ¼ cup Parmesan cheese (grated)
  - ¼ cup parsley (chopped)

Instructions:

- Using your Veggetti cutter, turn the zucchinis and carrots into narrow pasta strands. Heat or cook to your preferences.
- In a large pan, heat up the onion and celery until the onion begins to brown – 5 to 9 minutes.
- Stir in the Italian seasoning and garlic for about 45 seconds.
- Stir in the turkey, breaking it up as you go, and cook until it is no longer pink, inside or out – 4 to 6 minutes usually.
- Pour in the tomatoes and cook for another 4 to 6 minutes until they are

thickened. Add salt to taste.

- If you timed it right, the "pasta" should be done when the turkey and everything in the pan is finished. When that happens, carefully pour the sauce over the "pasta and dig in. This dish is less than 400 calories per serving and full of old world flavor.

Chinese Noodles & Chicken

Ingredients:

- "PASTA"
  - 2 large zucchinis
- SAUCE
  - ½ lb. boneless, skinless chicken (thin slices)
  - ½ cup rice wine
  - 1 tbsp soy sauce (reduced sodium)
  - 2 tsp light brown sugar
  - 4 tsp garlic-black bean sauce
  - 1 ½ tsp cornstarch
  - 4 tsp peanut oil
  - 1 tsp ginger (minced)
  - 1 small onion (sliced finely)
  - 5 cups Asian stir-fry vegetables (about 12 oz., fresh)
  - 1/2 cup water

Instructions:

- Using your Veggetti cutter, turn the zucchinis into narrow pasta strands. Heat or cook to your preferences.
- Mix brown sugar, rice wine, garlic-black bean sauce, cornstarch and soy sauce into a side bowl and let sit.
- In a large pan, heat 2 tsp of peanut oil over medium heat and add ginger and onion, cooking until they are soft – usually under 3 minutes.
- Combine Asian vegetables and ¼ cup of water and cook for 3 to 4 minutes until crisply tender, stirring every thirty seconds.
- Combine these vegetables, etc. with the noodles in the side bowl.
- Wipe any oil and vegetable residue from pan.
- Add the rest of the peanut oil to the pan and turn on medium-high heat.

- Add chicken slices and cook until the slices are brown and are not pink on the inside, 3 to 6 minutes.
- Pour the vegetables and the noodles and the rest of the water into the pan and stir and cook for another 4 to 6 minutes or until mixture is thoroughly heated.
- When ready, serve this wonderful weight loss version of a Chinese dish to your family and friends and just wait for the compliments to roll in.

Garlic Shrimp & Veggie Pasta

Ingredients:

- "PASTA"
  - 3 large zucchinis
- SAUCE
  - 12 oz. raw shrimp cut in 1-inch pieces (cleaned and de-veined)
  - 1 bell pepper (sliced thinly)
  - 1 bunch asparagus (thinly sliced and trimmed)
  - 1 cup peas (frozen or fresh)
  - 2 cloves garlic (minced)
  - 1 ½ cups plain yogurt (low or non-fat)
  - 1 tsp salt
  - ¼ cup parsley (finely chopped)
  - ¼ cup lemon juice
  - 1 tbsp extra-virgin olive oil
  - ½ tsp black pepper

Instructions:

- Your Veggetti cutter will make fast work of those 3 zucchinis and turn them into beautiful "pasta" strands, worthy of your favorite guests.
- Boil the veggie pasta for 1 minute and then add the shrimp, bell pepper, peas and asparagus to the water and cook another 4 to 6 minutes, or until the shrimp are cooked. Drain.
- Mix the salt and garlic together in a separate bowl until the texture is pasty.
- Add the parsley, lemon juice, yogurt, pepper and oil and whisk them all together.
- Add the pasta and all the rest to these ingredients and toss thoroughly.
- Now, you are in for a real treat. Serve and enjoy.

Creamy Chicken Pasta

Ingredients:

....

- "PASTA"
  - 1 large zucchini
  - 1 large carrots
- SAUCE
  - 3 slices bacon (turkey bacon is ok-chopped)
  - 1 tbsp canola oil
  - ½ lb. chicken breast (boneless & skinless-1 inch pieces)
  - 1 medium green bell pepper, sliced
  - 1 yellow onion (chopped)
  - 2 garlic cloves (crushed)
  - ½ black pepper
  - 1 tbsp flour (all-purpose)
  - 1 can crushed tomatoes (28-ounce)
  - 1/3 cup sour cream (reduced-fat)

....

Instructions:

- Using your Veggetti cutter, turn the carrots zucchinis into narrow pasta strands. Heat or cook to your preferences.
- Heat oil in pan over medium heat and add onion and bacon, cooking for 2 to 4 minutes until brown.
- Add bell pepper, garlic, chicken, and pepper. Cook about 4 minutes, until the bell pepper and onion begin to soften.
- Stir in flour to coat, then add the tomatoes and simmer for 4 to 6 minutes, until the chicken is thoroughly cooked and the sauce is bubbling up.
- Remove from heat and stir in sour cream. Stir in the sauce with the "pasta" and serve.

Pasta with Arugula & Italian Sausage

Ingredients:

- "PASTA"
  - 2 large carrots
- SAUCE
  - 1 large Italian turkey sausage (casing removed)
  - 2 tsp olive oil
  - 1 garlic clove (minced)
  - ½ cup cherry tomatoes (halved)
  - 2 cups arugula (spinach is ok)
  - 1/8 tsp salt
  - 1 tsp black pepper
  - ¼ cup Pecorino Romano or Parmesan cheese (finely shredded)

Instructions:

- Using your Veggetti cutter, turn the zucchinis into narrow pasta strands. Heat or cook to your preferences.
- Cook sausage in large pan over medium heat for 5 to 8 minutes, breaking it into small pieces as you stir.
- Mix in arugula, tomatoes and garlic and cook for another 2 to 4 minutes or until tomatoes start to break down. Cover and remove from heat.
- In a large bowl, mix the pepper, salt and cheese together and then pour in the left over cooking oil from the pan and combine thoroughly.
- Add the "pasta" and stir the mixture to combine all the ingredients.
- Top the "pasta" with the arugula and sausage mixture and serve.

Asian Pasta with Broth

Ingredients:

- "PASTA"
  - 2 large zucchinis
- SAUCE
  - ½ lb. lean ground turkey
  - 2 tbsp sesame oil (separated)
  - ½ cup sliced scallions
  - 2 garlic cloves (minced)
  - 1 tbsp fresh ginger (minced)
  - 2 cups chicken broth
  - ½ cup water
  - 1 tbsp rice vinegar
  - 2 tbsp soy sauce
  - 1 cups bok choy (thinly sliced)

Instructions:

- Using your Veggetti cutter, turn the zucchinis into narrow pasta strands. Heat or cook to your preferences.
- Cook the ground turkey in a pan with 1 tbsp oil over medium heat.
- Add garlic, ginger and most of the scallions, leaving 2 tbsp for later.
- Break up the turkey into small pieces as you cook everything for 5 to 8 minutes, until the turkey is no longer pink.
- Put on a plate and set aside.
- Combine water, broth, soy sauce, "pasta," vinegar, bok choy, into the pan with the left over oil and bring to a boil. Stir occasionally and cook for 3 to 5 minutes, until the "pasta is soft enough for you.
- Add the turkey mixture to this and stir to combine.

Greek Style Pasta

Ingredients:

- "PASTA"
  - 1 large zucchini
  - 1 large carrot
- SAUCE
  - 1 onion (chopped)
  - 2 garlic cloves (minced)
  - 2 tbsp olive oil (separated)
  - 1 bell pepper (chopped)
  - ½ tsp salt
  - ½ cup white wine (dry)
  - ½ cup feta cheese, (crumbled)
  - 1/8 tsp black pepper (to taste)
  - ¾ cup baby peas
  - ½ cup mint leaves (chopped)

Instructions:

- Using your Veggetti cutter, turn the zucchinis into narrow pasta strands. Heat or cook to your preferences.
- Brown the onion with 2 tsp of oil in a large pan for 3 to 5 minutes, and add some salt.
- Add the bell pepper to the onion and cook for another 3 minutes.
- Toss in the garlic and pour in the wine and cook until much of the wine has evaporated, about 2 to 4 minutes.
- Add the pasta to the pan, along with the peas, mint, and oil and feta cheese and stir well.
- Serve and be fulfilled.

Asian Chicken and Noodle Salad

Ingredients:

- "PASTA"
  - 2 large zucchinis
- SAUCE
  - ½ lb. skinless/boneless chicken breast (cut into small pieces)
  - 3 tbsp rice wine (low alcohol type)
  - 1/3 cup sesame-soy dressing (low calorie)
  - 1 tsp ginger (ground)
  - 1 tbsp sesame seeds (toasted)
  - ½ cup carrot (shredded)
  - 2 cups mixed salad greens

Instructions:

- Mix ginger and rice wine together in bowl, then marinate the chicken pieces with it in a baking dish. Set in refrigerator for half an hour.
- Using your Veggetti cutter, turn the zucchinis into narrow pasta strands. Heat or cook to your preferences.
- Put veggie pasta into a large bowl with carrot and sesame-soy dressing. Mix to coat the "pasta."
- Grill or broil the chicken pieces on a lightly oiled sheet for approximately10 minutes on each side, until the pink is gone. (Always make sure that the interior parts of the chicken reach at least 165° F, for safety).
- The salad is built from the bottom up, as you well know; first come the salad greens, then the "pasta" and then the chicken pieces. Top this delicious mixture with the remaining dressing and sprinkle sesame seeds over everything. Voila!

Zucchini Pasta & Turkey Sausage

Ingredients:

. . . .

- "PASTA"
  - 2 large zucchinis
- SAUCE
  - 1 Italian turkey sausage (casings removed)
  - 1 tbsp olive oil
  - 2 garlic cloves (minced)
  - 1 cup cherry tomatoes (halved)
  - 3 cups arugula (spinach is ok)
  - ¼ cup Pecorino Romano or Parmesan cheese (shredded)
  - 1 tsp black pepper (to taste)
  - ¼ tsp salt

. . . .

Instructions:

- Using your Veggetti cutter, turn the zucchinis into narrow pasta strands. Heat or cook to your preferences.
- Cook sausage in large pan over medium heat for at least 5 minutes, cutting it into small pieces as it cooks.
- Stir in arugula, tomatoes and garlic and cook until the greens are limp and the tomatoes start to break down, about 3 to 5 minutes. Cover and remove from heat.
- Mix the cheese, salt and pepper into a large bowl and stir in the residual cooking liquid from the pan. Add the "pasta" and toss to coat.
- Serve the "pasta" topped with the sausage and add more cheese if needed.

Fettuccine Alfredo Lite

Ingredients:

- "PASTA"
  - 1 large zucchini
  - 1 large carrot
- SAUCE
  - ½ cup plain Greek yogurt (non-fat)
  - ½ cup Parmesan cheese (shredded)
  - 1 tbsp butter
  - 1 garlic clove (minced)
  - 1 tbsp parsley (chopped)
  - ¼ tsp black pepper (to taste)
  - 1/8 tsp nutmeg (ground)
  - 1/8 tsp salt

Instructions:

- Using your Veggetti cutter, turn the zucchinis and carrots into narrow pasta strands. Heat or cook to your preferences. If you blanche or boil it, set aside ½ cup water after draining.
- In a large pan, melt the butter over medium heat and add the garlic. Cook for 1 to 2 minutes.
- Mix in the ½ cup water into the pan and then remove from heat.
- Stir in half the Parmesan cheese, and the salt, pepper, nutmeg and yogurt, along with the "pasta" and mix thoroughly.
- Serve with the rest of the Parmesan as topping.

***

RECIPES FOR GLUTEN-FREE (WHEAT-FREE) DIETS

Vegetable Pasta with Chicken Piccata

Ingredients:

- "PASTA"
  - 3 large zucchinis
  - 3 large carrots
- SAUCE
  - 4 chicken breast halves (medium size, skinless, boneless)
  - 1 cup cherry tomatoes, (halved)
  - 1 cup red bell pepper (1/4-inch strips)
  - 1½ cups chicken broth (fat free is suggested)
  - 1 ¼ cups yellow squash (matchstick-cut)
  - 2 garlic cloves (minced)
  - ¾ cup Parmesan cheese (grated)
  - ¾ cup onion (thinly sliced)
  - ¼ tsp salt
  - ½ cup fresh basil (thinly sliced)
  - 2 tsp olive oil
  - ½ cup flour (all-purpose)
  - 1 tbsp butter
  - 6 tbsp lemon juice
  - ½ cup green onions (sliced)
  - 2 tbsp capers

Instructions:

- Using your Veggetti cutter, turn the zucchinis and carrots into narrow pasta strands. Heat or cook to your preferences. Drain and save ½ cup of the pasta water for later.

- Over medium heat, sauté onion and bell pepper for 7 to 9 minutes or until they start to brown. Place these in a separate large bowl and set aside.

- Add squash to pan and sauté until tender crisp, about 4 minutes. Throw in the garlic and tomatoes and sauté another 2 minutes, stirring while it cooks. Add these sautéed ingredients to the onion mixture and stir them in.

- Add the "pasta" and saved water to the vegetable mix and combine. Add basil and1/2 cup Parmesan and stir. Keep warm.

- Salt and pepper the chicken on both sides and pour flour in a bowl. Fully coat the chicken with flour, and then shake off excess flour in the bowl.

- Coat a pan with olive oil and cook chicken over medium heat for 5 minutes on each side, or until chicken is done and there is no more pink, inside or outside of the meat. (Always make sure that the interior part of the chicken is at least 165° F before serving). Remove chicken from pan and keep it warm.

- Add juice, capers and broth to pan and bring to boil. Cook for 3 to 5 minutes, then remove from heat. Add the butter, black pepper and green onions to the pan and mix until the butter melts.

- Serve by placing "pasta" on plate first, then one breast of chicken, and then topping it with cheese and sauce.

Chicken Noodle Soup

Ingredients:

. . . .

- "PASTA"
  - 6 large carrots
- SAUCE
  - 1 - 3 ½ to 4 lb. chicken
  - 1 onion (large, quartered)
  - 4 celery stalks (sliced into I inch pieces)
  - 1 tsp black peppercorns
  - 2½ tsp salt

. . . .

Instructions:

- Wash the chicken inside and out and pat dry with paper towels. Put chicken in large pot.
- With your Veggetti cutter, transform 4 of the cleaned and peeled carrots into brilliant orange colored strands of "pasta."
- Clean and thinly slice two of the celery stalks and 2 of the carrot sticks and add those, along with the onion, peppercorns and salt into the pot with the chicken. Then add enough cold water to cover the chicken and all the ingredients and bring to a boil.
- Reduce the heat and let simmer for about 30 minutes or until the chicken is cooked thoroughly.
- Move the chicken to a separate bowl and let it cool.
- Strain the broth and put the vegetables and the strained broth back into the pot.
- When the chicken has cooled to the touch, pull the meat off and shred it into bite size sized pieces and put it back into the pot with the vegetables and broth.
- Scoop this hearty soup into individual bowls and enjoy.

Pork and Vegetables with Noodles

Ingredients:

- "PASTA"
  - 2 large zucchinis
- SAUCE
  - 3 boneless center-cut loin pork chops (cut into 1/4-inch strips)
  - 1 cup red bell pepper (thinly sliced)
  - 4 green onions
  - 1 tbsp sesame oil
  - 4 tsp chili garlic sauce {Check for Gluten}
  - 1/3 cup teriyaki sauce {Check for Gluten}
  - 3 ½ oz. shiitake mushrooms (sliced)

Instructions:

- Using your Veggetti cutter, turn the zucchinis into narrow pasta strands. Heat or cook to your preferences. Drain and save a ¼ cup of the pasta water for later use. Set aside "pasta" and keep it warm.
- Cut and slice the green onion tops and set aside.
- Mince the white portions only of the green onion and set aside.
- Add oil to a pan and heat over medium heat and add the minced onions, pork, mushrooms and bell pepper slices and sauté for 3 to 5 minutes or until pork is browned on both sides.
- Mix the saved pasta water, chili garlic sauce and teriyaki sauce in a small bowl and add it and the "pasta" to the pan. Toss thoroughly to coat and then stir in the sliced green onion tops and serve.

Pasta with Chicken in Creamy Tomato Sauce

Ingredients:

. . . .

- "PASTA"
  - 1 large zucchini
  - 1 large carrot
- SAUCE
  - 8 oz. chicken (boneless, skinless, cut into small pieces)
  - 2 garlic cloves (minced)
  - 1 cup cherry tomatoes (halved)
  - ½ onion (diced)
  - ½ cup fresh basil (slivered)
  - ½ cup coconut milk

. . . .

Instructions:

- Using your Veggetti cutter, turn the zucchinis and carrots into narrow pasta strands. Heat or cook to your preferences.
- In a pan, over medium heat, cook chicken pieces for 7 to10 minutes on each side, until there is no pink on the inside or outside. (Remember, make sure the interior of the chicken reaches a temperature of at least 165° F, for safety). Remove chicken and place in separate bowl.
- Cook the onions in the same pan for 3 to 5 minutes and then add the garlic and cook for another 1 to 2 minutes, until you can smell the garlic aroma. Add the tomatoes and cook for another 2 to 4 minutes.
- Add the coconut milk and bring the whole mixture to a boil until you see it thickening. Then put the chicken back into the pan and stir as it cooks for another 2 to 4 minutes.
- Serve the pan mixture over the pasta and sprinkle fresh basil over it and you're ready to go. Add coconut milk and bring to a boil, continuing to cook until saw has thickened a bit. Add ham back to the pan.
- Serve sauce over pasta, garnished with fresh basil.

Chicken Pesto Pasta

Ingredients:

- "PASTA"
  - 2 large zucchinis
  - 1 large carrot
- SAUCE
  - 2 cups chicken (shredded & pre-cooked)
  - 2 garlic cloves (minced)
  - 4 garlic cloves (thinly sliced)
  - 2 tbsp white wine
  - ½ onion (diced)
  - ¼ cup sliced almonds, dry toasted
  - 2 tbsp olive oil
  - ¼ cup vegan pesto
  - 1 cup coconut milk

Instructions:

- Using your Veggetti cutter, turn the zucchinis into narrow pasta strands. Heat or cook to your preferences.
- In a pan, over medium heat, cook the thinly sliced garlic for 4 to 6 minutes until they begin to brown, then remove from pan and drain on paper towels.
- Add onion and ginger to the still hot pan and cook for 3 to 6 minutes, until the onion turns translucent.
- Add the chicken pieces and cook for several minutes until brown on both sides. (Always cook chicken thoroughly. The interior of the chicken must reach at least 165° F for safety).
- Add the wine, coconut milk and pesto and stir. Simmer for 3 to 6 minutes as you reduce heat and stir.
- Serve the sauce over the "pasta" and top it with fried garlic, toasted

almonds and basil and you will be in heaven.

- Serve sauce with pasta, topped with toasted almonds, fried garlic and fresh basil.

Thai Salad with Chicken

Ingredients:

- "PASTA"
  - 2 large zucchinis
- CHICKEN
  - ½ rotisserie chicken (shredded)
  - 1 head Napa or Chinese cabbage (thinly sliced)
  - ¼ cup fresh cilantro (chopped)
  - 1 cucumber (matchstick cuts)
  - ¼ cup peanuts (chopped)
  - 3 green onions (chopped)
- DRESSING
  - 1 garlic clove (minced)
  - 2 tbsp peanut butter,
  - ¼ tsp sesame oil
  - 2 tbsp water
  - ½ tbsp lime juice
  - ½ red chili pepper (seeds removed, chopped)
  - ¼ tsp fish sauce
  - 1 tbsp tamari (gluten free)

Instructions:

- Using your Veggetti cutter, turn the zucchinis into narrow pasta strands. Heat or cook to your preferences.
- Whisk dressing ingredients together in a small bowl. Don't be afraid to taste it before you're finished mixing, as you may want to increase or decrease certain ingredients to your taste. Add water to thin the dressing.
- Mix all the salad ingredients in a large bowl and when it's complete, pour the dressing over the salad and you are ready to eat.

Pasta Carbonara — Lite

Ingredients:

- "PASTA"
  - 2 large zucchinis
  - 2 large carrots
- SAUCE
  - two eggs
  - 3 garlic cloves (minced)
  - ½ cup sharp cheddar cheese (shredded)
  - ¼ cup coconut milk
  - 5 oz. bacon
  - 1 tbsp capers
  - 4 green onions (sliced)
  - ½ onion (diced)
  - salt to taste
  - pepper to taste

Instructions:

- Cook the bacon until crispy in a pan over medium heat, then drain on paper towels. When cool, cut the bacon into small pieces and put into a bowl.
- Empty the pan of bacon grease and then add garlic and onions and cook for 2 to 4 minutes and remove from pan and put with the bacon pieces.
- In a separate bowl, combine the cheese, coconut milk, pepper, salt and eggs and mix until smooth.
- Warm or cook the zucchini and carrot pasta, then put back into pot.
- Pour in the egg mixture and stir to combine all the ingredients. Watch to be sure that the hot pot and "pasta" cooks the egg along with other ingredients.
- Mix in the onions, the bacon and the capers and you are ready to roll.

- Pour egg mixture over the pasta and mix quickly, making sure the pasta slightly cooks the egg mixture. Add in bacon and onions. Mix.
- Serve garnished with capers and green onions.

Pasta & Cheese with Bacon

Ingredients:

- "PASTA"
  - 2 large zucchinis
  - 1 large carrot
- SAUCE
  - 6 bacon slices (chopped)
  - ¼ cup heavy cream
  - 2 garlic cloves (minced)
  - salt to taste
  - pepper to taste
  - 6 oz. Gouda cheese (grated)
  - 8 oz. mozzarella, (grated)
  - ¼ cup fresh basil, slivered

Instructions:

- Using your Veggetti cutter, turn the zucchinis and carrots into narrow pasta strands. Heat or cook to your preferences.
- Cook bacon in a pan over medium heat. Just before the bacon is completed, add garlic and stir. Cook bacon until crispy.
- With bacon and garlic still in pan, add the pasta and heavy cream and reduce heat and stir until the cream is thick and starts to coat the pasta.
- Add the cheese and stir until it melts, then remove from heat and toss on some fresh basil and serve.

Pasta Salad — Italian Style

Ingredients:

- "PASTA"
  - 2 large zucchinis
  - 1 large carrot
- SALAD
  - ¼ cup cherry tomatoes (halved)
  - 4 oz. feta cheese (crumbled)
  - ¼ cup Basil (chopped)
  - ½ red pepper (chopped)
  - 2 green onions (chopped)
  - ¼ lb. deli salami (cubed)
- DRESSING
  - 1 ½ tsp dried oregano
  - 1/3 cup olive oil
  - 2 garlic cloves (minced)
  - 3 tbsp lemon juice
  - ½ tsp salt
  - ¼ tsp pepper

Instructions:

- Using your Veggetti cutter, turn the zucchinis into narrow pasta strands. Heat or cook to your preferences.
- Mix dressing ingredients together thoroughly with a whisk, then pour over combined and thoroughly tossed salad ingredients and serve.

Pasta Pie

Ingredients:

- "PASTA"
  - 3 large zucchinis
- SAUCE
  - 1 tablespoon olive oil
  - 1 ½ cups tomato sauce (half a 26-ounce jar)
  - ½ cup Parmesan cheese (grated gluten-free)
  - 5 fresh basil leaves
  - ½ cup mozzarella or Monterey Jack cheese (grated gluten-free)
  - ¼ cup black olives (sliced)
  - ½ cup bell pepper (sliced)

Instructions:

- Using your Veggetti cutter, turn the 3 zucchinis into fine strands of "pasta." No need to sauté or boil these for this recipe, as they will be making a visit to the oven tonight.
- Mix all ingredients in a large bowl, then place in an oven safe pan and bake for 30 minutes at 325°F.
- When done, remove from oven and let it cool down for 15 minutes. Then serve.

***

RECIPES FOR
A PALEO DIET

Sweet Potato Pasta

Ingredients:

- "PASTA"
  - 1 medium yam or sweet potato
- SAUCE
  - 2 tbsp olive oil
  - 1 tbsp sage
  - 1 tbsp cinnamon
  - sea salt to taste

Instructions:

- Make "pasta" strands out of the sweet potato with your Veggetti cutter.
- Heat olive oil in pan and add your sweet potato pasta noodles. Cook for 3 to 6 minutes until "pasta" is cooked to your taste.
- Season with cinnamon and sage and enjoy your low calorie and tasty "pasta" dish.

Sesame Noodles

Ingredients:

- "PASTA"
  - 4 medium sized zucchini
- SAUCE
  - 1/3 cup creamy roasted almond butter
  - 1 tbsp toasted sesame oil
  - 1 tbsp honey or agave nectar

Instructions:

- Make "pasta" out of the four zucchinis using the Veggetti.
- Combine almond butter, sesame oil and sweetener in a separate bowl.
- Mix noodles with sauce and serve.

Beet Pasta with Salmon

Ingredients:

- "PASTA"
  - 1 pound whole red and gold beets
- SAUCE
  - 1 tablespoon coconut oil
  - 1 medium onion, chopped
  - 3 garlic cloves, minced
  - 3 cups cauliflower florets
  - 1/3 cup lemon juice lemon juice
  - 1 ½ tablespoon lemon zest
  - 1 cup canned coconut milk
  - 1/2 tsp sea salt
  - 1/4 tsp black pepper
  - 1/2 tsp paprika
  - 1/2 tsp mustard powder
  - 1/2 tsp garlic powder
  - 1 tsp cumin
  - 2 (6-ounce) salmon fillets (wild caught)

Instructions:

- Remove the beet greens and cut the red and gold beets down to a size that fits into the Veggetti. The Cutter will slice them into "pasta" strands and then you can boil them for about 20 minutes or until soft.
- Sautee the onion for 4-6 minutes in coconut oil in a medium pan. Add garlic cloves and sauté for another minute.
- Steam cauliflower until tender, usually 5-7 minutes, then put in blender along with the garlic, onions, cumin, lemon juice and zest, coconut milk, pepper and salt. Liquefy until smooth.

- Preheat broiler and line a cookie sheet with aluminum foil.

- Sprinkle mixture of mustard powder, salt, paprika, cumin, salt and garlic powder over salmon and lay it on the foil. Bake for 8 minutes or until the salmon is thoroughly cooked and flakey and the internal temperature is at least 140° F.

- Pour blended sauce into saucepan and heat for 2 minutes, then pour over pasta on serving plate. Salmon can be served next to or on top of "pasta."

Zucchini Pasta with Avocado Sauce

Ingredients:

- "PASTA"
  - 4 medium sized zucchini
- SAUCE
  - 1 avocado (ripe)
  - 1/2 a cucumber, sliced
  - ¼ cup lemon juice
  - 1 clove crushed garlic
  - 2 tbsp coconut milk (or almond milk)
  - Pepper and salt

Instructions:

- Make "pasta" strands out of the zucchini with your Veggetti. Heat or cook as you prefer.
- Combine and blend the rest of the ingredients until texture is smooth.
- Mix the zucchini "pasta" and sauce thoroughly, season with salt and pepper and serve.

Carrot Pasta

Ingredients:

- "PASTA"
  - 3 large carrots
- SAUCE
  - 3 tsp olive oil
  - 1/4 tsp salt
  - Black pepper (pinch)
  - ¾ cup chopped mushrooms
  - 2 tbsp finely chopped onion or shallot
  - 3/4 tsp basil (dried)
  - 1 tbsp minced garlic

Instructions:

- Make "pasta" strands out of the carrots with your Veggetti. Set aside.
- Add onion, or shallots and garlic to heated oil in medium pan and sauté for 2-3 minutes.
- Sprinkle pepper, salt, mushrooms and basil into pan and heat for 6-7 minutes or until mushroom liquid is gone.
- Add the carrot "pasta" and sauté for 2 minutes, then add the sauce and mix thoroughly.
- Cook everything for 7-9 more minutes or until the "pasta" is tender enough for your taste. Serve and enjoy!

Paleo Zucchini Pasta with Chicken

Ingredients:

"PASTA"

- 8 medium zucchinis
- SAUCE
  - 1 lb. boneless chicken breast
  - 3 tbsp. coconut oil
  - 1/4 cup sun-dried tomatoes, chopped
  - 1/4 cup virgin olive oil
  - 3½ oz. of sliced black olives (canned)
  - 1/3 cup pine nuts (sliced or slivered almonds okay)
  - ¼ cup lemon juice
  - 1 tsp. garlic powder
  - Zest from ½ lemon
  - 1 tsp. arrowroot powder (thickening agent)
  - pepper and salt to taste

Instructions:

- Using the Veggetti cutter, make pasta strands out of the 8 zucchinis. Heat or cook as you prefer.
- Slice chicken into small chunks and pieces and then season with pepper, salt and garlic powder.
- In a medium pan, heat the coconut oil and then put in the chicken pieces and sear for 5-7 minutes. Reduce heat and simmer chicken until cooked thoroughly.
- Add olives, pine nuts, sun-dried tomatoes, arrowroot powder, lemon zest and juice, once chicken is done.
- Simmer all ingredients until hot, then turn heat off and add the olive oil.
- Stir to mix, then serve over pasta.

Pesto Pasta & Sausages

Ingredients:

- "PASTA"
  - 3 medium zucchinis
- SAUCE
  - 1 Cup fresh basil leaves
  - 1/4 Cup Walnuts
  - 1/4 Cup Almonds
  - 5 to 6 cloves garlic
  - 1 Red Bell Pepper (diced)
  - 3 Tablespoons Extra Virgin Olive Oil
  - Salt to taste
  - 1 cup (when cut) spiced chicken sausages (or your choice of flavor)

Instructions:

- Using the Veggetti cutter, make pasta strands out of the zucchinis. Heat or cook as you prefer.
- Toast nuts for 3 to 4 minutes, then, when cool, mix them with the basil, oil, garlic and salt in a blender until they are a smooth paste.
- Cut sausages into small ¾ inch pieces and cook them in a pan with oil.
- When everything is fully cooked, mix the zucchini pasta, bell pepper and the sausages and smother it with the pesto sauce.
- If you're up for it, frost it with Extra Virgin Olive Oil and sliced olives!

Carrot and Zucchini Spaghetti with Olive Oil

Ingredients:

- "PASTA"
  - 2 large zucchinis
  - 2 large carrots
- SAUCE
  - 3 cloves garlic (crushed)
  - Pinch of salt (to taste)
  - 2 ½ cups spinach leaves (finely chopped)
  - 1/3 cup pumpkin seeds
  - ¼ cup olive oil

Instructions:

- Use your Veggetti cutter to transform the zucchini and carrots into "spaghetti." You can leave them raw, if you prefer, or steam, sauté, boil or blanche them for several minutes until soft.
- The spinach leaves, salt, garlic, pumpkin seeds and olive oil should be blended thoroughly together and poured over the vegetable "spaghetti" for a marvelously low calorie plate of "pasta."

Lemon Zest & Black Pepper Tagliatelle

(Tagliatelle are simply long, flat strands of "pasta" that resemble fettuccine pasta.)

Ingredients:

- "PASTA"
  - 3 large zucchinis
- SAUCE
  - 3 tbsp olive oil
  - 3 cloves garlic (crushed)
  - Pinch of salt (to taste)
  - 1/3 cup pumpkin seeds
  - Zest from ½ lemon
  - ½ tsp black pepper

Instructions:

- Use your Veggetti cutter to make wide pasta ribbons out of the zucchinis. Heat or cook as you prefer.
- Put pepper, lemon zest, olive oil, pumpkin seeds, salt and garlic in blender until it has a smooth texture.
- Serve "pasta" on a plate and drizzle blended sauce over it. This is actually a deliciously simple and quick dish to make. You may want to use less pepper at first and then add more per taste.

Rosemary & Tomato Pasta

Ingredients:

- "PASTA"
- 4 large zucchinis
- 2 large carrots
- SAUCE
- ½ yellow onion (finely chopped)
- 1 tsp rosemary (dried and crushed)
- 4 garlic cloves (crushed)
- Pepper and salt to taste
- ¼ cup olive oil
- 1 large can of stewed, whole tomatoes (drained and finely chopped)

Instructions:

- Using your Veggetti cutter, turn the zucchinis into narrow pasta strands. Heat or cook to your preferences.
- In a blender or large bowl, add the tomatoes, garlic, salt, pepper, rosemary, onion and olive oil and blend until smooth.
- Put blended ingredients into a medium saucepan and heat over a medium flame for 8-10 minutes.
- The "pasta" is ready to be put on your favorite dish and just waiting for this absolutely delicious sauce to be poured over it.

WHAT'S NEXT?

I hope this short book has been as delicious and "nutrient-packed" for you as the recipes you're beginning to explore. Often, it takes a gentle nudge from a book like this to help people discover the delicious benefits of "veggie pasta", and of a diet consisting of mostly unprocessed or unrefined foods. If this book has helped you take a step or two in that direction, then let me know! Send me an email and tell me what you think of this book. What's great about it? What benefits did you get from trying some of the recipes? Can the book or the recipes be improved? What's missing?

I see this book, and others in my series on healthy foods, as a journey toward better health, more energy, and ultimately a greater experience of life. Let's take this journey together!

Visit my website (www.HealthyHappyFoodie.org) and sign up for a free audiobook version of this Kindle book, and for other free books, videos and content. I'm an independent, self-published author,

And, leave a review on Amazon! Reviews are the lifeblood of independent authors like myself. The more honest reviews, the better... even if it's a bad review, at least it will give me some feedback and direction so the next version of this book can be better.

Thank you for reading!

J.S. Amie

ABOUT THE AUTHOR

J.S. Amie is "the Healty Happy Foodie" -- an Amazon bestselling author who is quickly building a name as a trusted source for delicious recipes which support amazing health and happiness. Her books on dieting, cleansing, smoothies, Paleo lifestyle, low carb and healthy ice cream are gaining popularity with a wide variety of people who all share the same passion for eating well while staying healthy.

She is a mother of two charming daughters, who, like normal children, crave sugar, wheat and more sugar! So what to do? JS decided to learn about how to satisfy those urges by substituting good, natural food for unhealthy junk. Her books reflect her personal mission to nourish her family as well as possible. She lives in a small town surrounded by rolling hills, walnut trees and zombies. Just kidding about the zombies.

Other Titles By J. S. Amie

- **How To Use Coconut Oil For Health**: A Practical Guide for Improving Skin and Hair with Coconut Oil!
- **Critical Smoothie Ingredients for Better Health**: Delicious Green Smoothie Recipes to Lose Weight, Cleanse Your Body, and Re-Energize Your Life

WOULD YOU LIKE TO HELP MORE PEOPLE SEE THIS BOOK?

Then please consider giving a review! It's easy…just go the end of this book on your Kindle or tablet and a review prompt will automatically appear. Or, go to the book's page on Amazon and click the "Write a Customer Review" button near the review chart.

Customer reviews are the lifeblood of independent authors like me. I look at reviews very carefully to know how people like my book. And a review lets other people know whether to buy the book or not. Please take a quick minute to write an honest review, I would be very grateful.

J.S. Amie

LEGAL DISCLAIMER

As a self-published author, and due to the litigious times we live in, I must state very clearly that I make no claim about the accuracy or reliability of any information contained in this book. This book is for entertainment purposes only. The views expressed are those of the author alone, and should not be taken as expert instruction or commands. You, the reader, are responsible for your own actions.

The information contained in this book is the opinion of the author and is based on the author's personal experience and observations. The author does not assume any liability whatsoever for the use of or inability to use any or all information contained in this book, and accepts no responsibility for any loss or damages of any kind that may be incurred by the reader as a result of actions arising from the use of information in this book. Use this information at your own risk.

The author reserves the right to make any changes he or she deems necessary to future versions of the publication to ensure its accuracy.

**

NOTES